T0193537

The Happiest Day for Simeon and Sula

Pamela Alarcon

Illustrator: Ochu Eddy Sheggy

Inspiring Voices books may be ordered through booksellers or by contacting:

Inspiring Voices
1663 Liberty Drive
Bloomington, IN 47403
www.inspiringvoices.com
1 (866) 697-5313

Because of the dynamic nature of the Internet, any web addresses or links contained in this book may have changed since publication and may no longer be valid. The views expressed in this work are solely those of the author and do not necessarily reflect the views of the publisher, and the publisher hereby disclaims any responsibility for them.

Any people depicted in stock imagery provided by Getty Images are models, and such images are being used for illustrative purposes only. Certain stock imagery © Getty Images.

Interior Image Credit: Ochu Eddy Sheggy

ISBN: 978-1-4624-1306-5 (sc)
ISBN: 978-1-4624-1307-2 (e)

Print information available on the last page.

Inspiring Voices rev. date: 08/27/2020

Hello! My name is Simeon. I am 8 years old. This is my sister Sula. She is 7. We live in a small village in Tanzania Africa. Our village is located near a great big mountain called Mount Kilimanjaro.

My family lives in a house. Our house is made out of mud, cow dung and small pieces of wood. Our roof top is made from grasses. My whole family lives in this house: my dad, mom, sister, grandparents and several cousins. My house has one room. We huddle together at night to sleep and share blankets to stay warm. There is no electricity or running water and our kitchen is outside of our house.

Every morning my mama wakes Sula and me before the sun is up and before we hear the rooster crow. Our daily chore is to take a bucket one for each hand and walk to the river. This is our only water source. The river is many miles from our house. It is dark outside when we leave. We have to be careful because wild animals roam around. We stop many times on our walk because we are tired, thirsty and hungry. We have very little to eat or drink at home so we find some grasses or a piece of fruit to eat along the way to keep our tummies from hurting.

When we arrive at the river, dozens of people from nearby villages are there waiting to get their water too. We also meet the Masai people with their animals. All of us need water, including the animals, so we must share what is in the river. Sula and I push hard to get to the front of the line. People are not happy because they have also had to walk very far to get to this river.

We pass many children who are wearing school uniforms and carrying cloth school bags. Sula and I stop and watch them walk happily to school. We wonder if there will ever be a day when we can go like the other children. I whisper to Sula, "Maybe one day, you and I will no longer have to carry these buckets but rather we will carry school bags and exercise books for school." We look at each other and with a deep sigh begin our journey home.

After Sula and I have filled our buckets, we begin to walk home. The buckets are heavy. Sula keeps asking me: "Simeon can we rest?" The sun has now come up and it's shining very bright. It is also very hot. We are hungry. We have been up more than five hours and have walked many miles to get this water. I tell Sula, "we must keep walking, Mama is waiting for us to bring the water back."

Mama was waiting patiently for us to arrive home. She had been taking care of my grandparents and my cousins while we did our chores. This water is so important to our family. My dad uses it to water our corn. Mama begins to boil a large pot of this water. We use this to wash dishes, cook and if there is water left, we will take a light bath. Mama will add cornmeal to this water for our lunch. This food is called "ugali." We love ugali. It is one of our favorite foods. We can roll it into a ball and use it as a spoon to scoop up vegetables if we have those to eat. Our family will sit together to eat. Mama always has us say our prayers and give thanks for everything we have before we take a bite of our food.

My dad grows a few stalks of corn in the nearby field. He takes it to market to sell when they are ready. We do not have grocery stores where we live so we sell our goods to each other. My Dad will earn 50 cents from selling his corn. We have one banana tree by our house and Mama sells the bananas at the market too. She will earn $1 for all of her bananas. This is all the money our family will have for a week, or even longer.

It is now late in the afternoon and we are tired. My feet have many sores on them from walking every day. We don't have money for shoes so Sula and I sometimes find cornhusks and wrap them around our feet. It helps a little bit to keep the pebbles and rocks away from our skin. My mama said she will try to find a job on a local farm to get some extra money for our family. We appreciate our parents so much!

Sula and I help my mama take her bananas to market on Tuesdays. We carry bunches of bananas on our heads, just like she does. We walk many miles to get to the market. While my mama sells her bananas, Sula and I decide to wander around. There is a school that we wanted to visit to see what the classrooms looked like. As we hide behind the bushes, we hear some people talking. They are talking about food that will be coming to this building. Sula asks me: "Simeon do you think we will get to have a meal or will this only be for the school children and their families?" I am not sure so I go running to Mama to ask her. She is so excited but says we will have to wait and be patient. I say, "Mama my belly is so hungry and it hurts all the time." She says: "Simeon, I believe there are very kind and generous people in our world, let us have hope that we will get help soon."

Our neighbors are talking about somebody who wants to help our village, and the many children and families who are hungry. Sula and I are beginning to have hope. We don't eat every day. We might have ugali once every two days or when Mama and Dad have a few extra coins to purchase the cornmeal. Ugali has no flavor. It tastes like the bark from a tree, but when Mama makes this food, my belly feels full for a little while.

One day as Mama is waking us up to go to the river for water, Sula began to cry. She says: "Mama my head is burning up and I am sweating." I tell her to stay back and I will go and get the water myself. Mama is very concerned about Sula. She takes some wet cloths and puts them on Sula's head to try to cool her down. As I walk, I know there is something wrong with Sula she is very sick and we have no doctors in our village. I return home to find her very weak. She needs food; her body is so hungry. I run everywhere asking people to find something for Sula to eat.

Our neighbor up the hill shouts to me: "Simeon, please get your family to the primary school." I reply, "Why go to this school?" My neighbor explains that his wife was asked to come early in the morning to prepare hundreds of meals in the outdoor kitchen. Food had arrived for the children in our village. I remember the day Sula and I overheard the people talking at the school about some food that was coming. My neighbor tells me, "the school will help you and your family. Get there soon they will be serving a meal at three p.m."

I ran home and told my family the news. Sula was so weak and I had no energy left. My Dad wrapped Sula in a blanket and carried her. My mama took my hand and guided me too. We walked to the school and there were hundreds of people standing in a long line. I ran to the front of the line and explained that my sister was very ill because of starvation. They allowed my family to be first through the door and to be seated at the table. The others filed in quickly and they began to pass out bowls of food. This food was magic. We began to eat rice, beans and vegetables. It tasted so good. You could have heard a cow moo or a chicken clucking. It was so quiet with everyone filling their hungry bellies!

At the end of our meal, a caring and kind lady from our village stood in the front and explained that there were many wonderful people from the USA who cared so much for us. She explained that one person came to see how we lived and went back and began to share the story. People saw through her pictures and stories that the need in our village and country was huge and immediately began to help her. She began to send money to purchase the food that so many needed.

I could not believe my ears! Everyone in this building began clapping, singing, dancing and even crying. I watched my parents as they bowed their head and said many prayers of thanks for this news. My imagination was going wild! To imagine if our bodies had better nutrition, I would be stronger, healthier and I might be able to go to school! Sula even began to smile when she heard the news. Although she was still very weak, knowing we had this delicious food waiting for us made everyone happy.

The days and weeks flew by. My whole family went to receive our meals every day. My muscles were getting stronger and stronger. Sula regained her smile and became well quickly. The same kind people who provided the food – were also going to teach us basic gardening and ways to care for our chickens, goats and other animals. Now our village could join together to grow, share and help others to receive more! All because one person decided to simply help us.

After several months our hunger began to disappear. We planted our seeds as we were taught. We grew corn, beans, carrots, onions, peppers and spinach. We planted more banana and mango trees too! We were now able to take our extra crops to market, earn a little more money and best of all we could feed our own family. Our chickens were laying eggs and multiplying. Our goats were being used for their milk and we could share the new offspring that were being born. Mama was busier than ever. She had so much to do – but was able to help our family grow and become stronger.

The best news of all was that Sula and I could finally go to school. My family had saved enough money to buy uniforms and pay our school fees. Although we were starting school at ages 8 and 9, we were now strong enough to learn. Education would help us in so many ways. We would learn to read, write, add and subtract.

It is because someone cared enough to help that me, my sister Sula and my whole family are now ready for the future. We do not have to rely on others but now we can provide for those that might not have what they need. We are so grateful and know that love is all it takes to make this world a better place. This is the happiest day for us.

The End

GLOSSARY

Banana Tree: A treelike tropical plant bearing thick clusters of yellow or reddish fruit that is full of vitamins.

Bucket: Cylindrical open container typically made of metal or plastic, with a handle, used to hold and carry liquids or other materials

Cloth School Bag: A Bag for carrying school books and supplies.

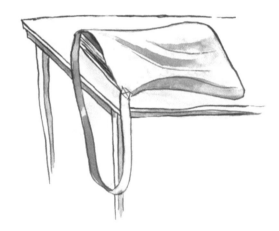

Corn Husk Shoes: Loose corn husks from the corn plant that might be wrapped around the feet to protect from small pebbles and dirt.

Mango Tree: The evergreen Indian tree of the cashew family that bears a fleshy oval, yellowish and tropical fruit that is eaten ripe or used green for pickles or chutneys.

Masai: A tribe of people that are pastoral and live off the land. They move frequently with their livestock and build temporary homes as they move around the country of Tanzania. They are known for their bright red, blue and purple blankets that they wear to protect from the wind and environment.

Mount Kilimanjaro: Tallest mountain in Africa and is located in Tanzania. It is a dormant volcanic mountain with three cones. This mountain is 19, 341 feet.

Outdoor Kitchen: Typically, small wood structure with grass or tin roof. Stove might have three main stones with firewood in the middle and can hold a large cooking pot. Wood sticks or spoons will stir food in cooking pot.

Primary School: Elementary age children attend primary school if their families can afford a uniform, school fees and school supplies. An average uniform costs $15.00, shoes $10.00 and school fees and supplies $100.00. The typical classroom will have 30-40 students and all students share desks and chairs.

Rooster: An adult male domestic chicken

Tanzania home: Typical village home made of cow dung, mud and sticks. The roof is made out of grasses which are layered to protect the inside of the home. A home consists of one room where entire families will sleep on the ground.

Village Market Stand: Families that grown produce take to a market to sell. A market stand can hold many fruits, vegetables and other items. It is made out of wood and metal.

ABOUT THE ILLUSTRATOR

Ochu Eddy Sheggy lives in Dar es Salaam Tanzania Africa. He was orphaned at age 11 and was not able to continue his education due to lack of family and financial support. He discovered that drawing helped his heart from hurting with the loss of both of his parents. "Ochu" was an only child and became a street kid at an early age. He would wait for students in school to give him their used pencils and paper so he could draw. His talent was discovered as author Pamela Alarcon was meeting with a friend of "Ochu" upon one of her visits to Tanzania Africa. Her manuscript was read to him and he began to cry. The story that Pamela writes depicts a very similar story from the beginning of his life. He used the few art supplies that were given to him and together they have combined their efforts to depict firsthand what this story is all about. Ochu is also a talented musician. He plays guitar, sings and composes music.

ABOUT THE AUTHOR

Pamela Alarcon a native of the mid-west grew up in a wholesome community surrounded by a wonderful family. Her desire to help others began at an early age. She has always had an open heart to welcome anyone into her home. Growing up, her family hosted many foreign exchange students and she always wanted to learn about their cultures and families. She has immersed herself into various mission outreaches from helping the homeless to helping others learn about their faith. God had a big plan for her life and that plan unfolded In February 2009. She took a life changing trip to Tanzania East Africa. It was during this trip she was faced with the reality of how others in developing nations live.

In Simeon and Sula's Happiest Day, African traveler and humanitarian Pamela Alarcon weaves a story of harsh realities and attainable dreams – dreams made possible by her commitment to "Love one another as I have loved you" John 13:34-35 Her focus has always focused on feeding the economically destitute but also include a component of teaching them to be sustainable for their future. She continues to serve Tanzania and her work can be found on her website: www. missionbarista.com The motto of Mission Barista is: "Helping people Changing lives" and The Happiest Day for Simeon and Sula, Alarcon creates a place for the reader to learn how others live in Africa.

Alarcon simply offers young readers an unforgettable glimpse into a world of hardship – but also hope says Simeon.

"We are so grateful and know that love is all it takes to make this world a better place. This is the happiest day for us."

Printed in the United States
By Bookmasters